CAN YOU SURVIVE

DEADLY

RAIN FOREST

ENCOUNTERS?

An Interactive
Wilderness Adventure

by Allison Lassieur

Published by Capstone Press, an imprint of Capstone
1710 Roe Crest Drive, North Mankato, Minnesota 56003
capstonepub.com

Library of Congress Cataloging-in-Publication Data is available on the Library of
Congress website.
ISBN: 9781666337884 (hardcover)
ISBN: 9781666337891 (paperback)
ISBN: 9781666337907 (ebook PDF)
Library of Congress Control Number: 2022943725

Summary: Could you survive being trapped in a rain forest? Imagine a run-in with a
poison dart frog in the Amazon Rain Forest, a chimpanzee in the African Congo, or a
clouded leopard in the jungles of Southeast Asia. How far would you be willing to go to
save your own life? Would it work? Flip through these pages to find out!

Editorial Credits
Editor: Mandy Robbins; Designer: Heidi Thompson; Media Researchers: Jo Miller and
Pam Mitsakos; Production Specialist: Tori Abraham

Image Credits
Alamy: Martin Harvey, 64, Pacific Imagica, 88; Getty Images: danikancil, 84,
davidsuarez82, 68, Tanaonte, 105, Teddy_Winanda, 80, Warmlight, 86; Shutterstock:
Antonin Vinter, Cover, defpicture, design element, throughout, Ecopix, 83, Elaine Smart
-Di Battista, 75, FABRIZIO CONTE, 73, Jess Kraft, 35, MiroArt, 52, Patrick K.
Campbell, 16, photoinnovation, 9, Ryan M. Bolton, 21, Sergey Uryadnikov, 56, 96, Tatiana
Belova, 30, Teo Tarras, 13, The Road Provides, 47, Travel Stock, 112, Tristan Barrington,
27, ylq, 60

TABLE OF CONTENTS

LOST IN THE RAIN FOREST!

YOU find yourself stranded in the middle of the rain forest. Threats lurk everywhere. You're hot. You're sweaty. And most terrifying of all, deadly wildlife could creep out at every turn. Snakes, big cats, gorillas, and more. You never know what you might find—or what might find you.

What will you do when you come face-to-face with a deadly rain forest creature? Will you run? Will you hide? Do you have what it takes to survive? YOU CHOOSE which paths to take. Your choices will guide the story and decide—will you live or die?

• Turn the page to begin your adventure.

CHAPTER 1

WILD ENCOUNTERS IN THE JUNGLE

You have always dreamed of visiting a rain forest. You imagine sharp-toothed tigers lurking about. Chattering monkeys swing through vine-covered trees. The buzz of insects echoes in the air around exotic plants you've never seen before. You can almost feel the humidity and smell the sweet scents of fruits and flowers that are all new to you.

• Turn the page.

More than half the world's original rain forests have been destroyed. Humans have cut them down for farmland, logging, and mining. Many people are working to save the rain forests. They're protecting endangered animals and finding uses for rain forest plants.

As humans push deeper into rain forests, animal encounters happen more often. It's smart to know what to do when you encounter a wild animal. It can mean the difference between life and death.

There's one important rule to remember. Don't do anything that will cause the animal to change its behavior. Watch to see if an animal growls, bares its teeth, stomps, cries out, or backs away. If so, it is likely stressed or afraid. If you see any of these behaviors, keep your distance. You're more likely to have an exciting, danger-free encounter.

You finally have the chance to begin your own rain forest adventure. You understand the dangers. You think you're ready for whatever you might encounter. Where will you choose to go?

- To search for a lost city in the Amazon jungle, turn to page 11.
- To hunt down rare medicinal plants in the Congo rain forest in Africa, turn to page 37.
- To look for the Sumatran serow, an endangered rain forest animal, turn to page 67.

CHAPTER 2

ON THE HUNT FOR A LOST CITY

Stories of the ancient Inca civilization have always excited you. Your favorite is the legend of Paititi, the mysterious Gold City. According to old stories, the Incas stored gold and jewels in this hidden city. Many people have searched for it. No one has found it. Now it's your turn to try. This trip won't be easy. You'll face thick jungles, extreme weather, and deadly wildlife. You think you're ready for the challenge.

• Turn the page

Your adventure starts in Cusco, Peru. From there, your guides take you deep into the Amazon Rain Forest. You drive for several days along narrow dirt roads.

You and your team finally arrive in a small village. It will be your base camp. From here, you'll decide where to start the search.

There are two promising leads to explore. One is a mountain in the jungle. Local hunters report a huge Inca ruin on the mountaintop. But it's several days' hike away. The other is a report of a mysterious rock carving. But the only way to find it is by boat. Which will you choose?

- To join the group that will explore the mountain, turn to page 14.
- To go with the group that will head down the river, turn to page 24.

13

You've been hiking through the jungle for a couple of days. The only path is a narrow, muddy track crowded with plants. Everyone is sticky with sweat. Your hands are covered with stinging cuts from thorny plants and rough branches.

On the third day, a thunderstorm hits. Your food and gear are soaked. Everyone is tired and discouraged. The team makes camp early. But you want to explore more. You mark their location on your GPS and continue on alone.

After awhile, you trip on something hard. A large stone is sticking out of the mud. Maybe it's part of the city ruins! As you bend down to take a look, a spider monkey drops from a tree. It grabs your GPS! It will be hard to find base camp again without it.

- To follow the monkey into the jungle, go to page 15.
- To stay where you are, turn to page 20.

You have to get your **GPS** back!
The monkey swings deeper into the jungle.
You chase it through the underbrush.
Hopefully, it will drop it and you can get
back to camp.

The jungle is too thick, and the monkey is
too fast. It finally disappears into the canopy.
Breathing hard, you stop. You realize it's
getting dark. Even worse, you don't know
where you are. Panic washes over you.

The first rule of being lost is to stay where
you are. But you don't want to spend the night
in the jungle alone. Maybe you can get back
to camp.

• To try to find your camp, turn to page 16.
• To stay where you are, turn to page 17.

You left a trail of broken branches and vines while chasing the monkey. You follow it back the way you came. You expect to see the camp soon.

As the sun goes down, you pull a flashlight from your backpack. Good thing, because you almost trip over a long, thick tree root. Just as you step over it, it moves! Suddenly, you feel a sharp pain on your ankle. This isn't a tree root. It's a bushmaster, the largest and most venomous snake in the rain forest. Their venom is so strong that it can kill a human in only a few minutes. Unfortunately, that's you.

THE END

To follow another path, turn to page 11.
To learn more about life in the rain forest, turn to page 101.

To survive the night, you'll need food, water, shelter, and some kind of weapon. You empty your backpack. You've got two bottles of water, a handful of energy bars, a flashlight, a rain poncho, and a pocketknife. It's not much, but it might just be enough.

By now, it's dark, and you need to build a shelter. But you're so tired. You could simply wrap up in the poncho and sleep under a nearby tree.

• To sleep under the tree, turn to page 18.
• To build a shelter, turn to page 19.

You gulp down some water and eat a couple of energy bars. Then you curl up at the base of the tree. Soon you're snoring.

Blinding pain jerks you awake! You're covered with huge black ants. These must be bullet ants! Each one is more than an inch long. They have the world's most painful sting. Their venom causes paralysis, so you can't move. You pass out from the terrible pain.

The next morning, your team finds you. You barely remember being carried back to camp. It can take up to 24 hours for the pain from a single bullet ant sting to go away. You've been stung dozens of times. You're not going anywhere until you recover. Your rain forest adventure is over.

THE END

To follow another path, turn to page 11.
To learn more about life in the rain forest, turn to page 101.

You build a small lean-to with branches and large leaves. You wrap up in the poncho. You try to ignore the loud scratching noises on the roof over your head.

At dawn, you're awakened by someone calling your name. Your friends have found you! You scramble out of the lean-to. To your horror, there are several hairy tarantulas crawling around the roof! One spider is the size of a dinner plate.

They're no danger to humans, but they are scary to look at. Quickly, you grab your backpack and head toward the shouting. Hopefully, this will be your closest—and last—encounter with these giant spiders.

THE END

To follow another path, turn to page 11.
To learn more about life in the rain forest, turn to page 101.

You want your **GPS** back. But you're not going to chase a monkey in the rain forest to get it. If you stay on the trail, you should be able to find your way back to camp.

Now, about this stone. You dig it out of the mud. It's cut into a perfect square. Maybe this was part of an ancient Inca road? Nearby, you uncover a piece of a wall. You're so excited that you almost miss a flash of neon green that jumps off the stone wall. A tiny, green-striped frog is sitting on a large vine.

• To inspect the frog more closely, go to page 21.
• To go tell your teammates about your discovery, turn to page 23.

This might be a poison frog. These frogs have powerful poison right on their skin. It could kill several humans. But their poison is only dangerous if it gets into your bloodstream. Touching the frog shouldn't be a problem. You gently pick it up and take several photos.

• Turn the page.

A few minutes later, you start to feel sick to your stomach. You are not sure how the poison got into your bloodstream. Then you notice fresh scrapes on your hands. You stumble toward the camp, shaking and throwing up as you go. You're miserably sick through the night, but you make it. The next morning, you're weak but glad to be alive. The team pushes deeper into the rain forest.

This trip is cursed with bad luck. Terrible rainstorms ruin your supplies. Several others fall sick from insect bites. The team is stuck in the jungle for days. Food runs low. You have no choice. The team decides to abandon the expedition and go back to the village. You hope the other team had better luck.

THE END

To follow another path, turn to page 11.
To learn more about life in the rain forest, turn to page 101.

The team is impressed that you saw a poison frog. But they're even more excited about the ruins you found. The next day, you show them the stone and wall. You agree that they are part of the great Inca road system.

The Inca built thousands of miles of stone roads through the rain forest. This system connected cities and villages. It allowed the Incas to easily carry goods and messages from place to place.

The rain forest is filled with the ruins of these roads. You hope one of them will lead to Paitili.

THE END

To follow another path, turn to page 11.
To learn more about life in the rain forest, turn to page 101.

You're dying to see the rock carving! The first day of the trip is beautiful. The weather is great and the water smooth. That night, you make camp just in time. Thunderstorms begin. Blue lightning flashes through the jungle. Thunder shakes the tents. The next morning, the river has swollen to twice its size.

The guides have a tough time steering the boats in the fast, swirling water. Around noon, you reach a bend in the river. Piles of trees and brush clog the water. The team has a choice. You can try to paddle around the blockage. Or empty the boats and carry everything along the bank.

• To paddle around the logjam, go to page 25.
• To carry the boats and supplies overland, turn to page 29.

It takes several hours, but the guides carefully push the boats past the logs. Everyone is relieved when you continue on your way.

As the sun begins to set, your guide points to something in the water. It's a pink river dolphin! These beautiful mammals only live in freshwater rivers in the Amazon Rain Forest. It's very rare to see pink dolphins. You grab your phone and take photos.

Finally, the group lands. It's time to make camp. You'd like to get one more peek at a pink dolphin before dark. But the guides warn you that deadly caiman lurk along the riverbank. These alligators are the largest predators in the Amazon. But there's still some daylight left. You tell your group that you would spot a black caiman before it would see you. And you won't be gone long.

• To go to the riverbank, turn to page 26.
• To stay in camp, turn to page 27.

You scan the river for signs of the dolphins, but none appear. You stand there until it's too dark to see. So you switch on your flashlight and head back to camp.

As you step away from the water, the light catches eyes staring at you. Before you realize what is happening, a black caiman rushes toward you. It clamps down on your leg.

Your screams alert your team. They run to help you. One of the guides kills the caiman, while the others carry you back to camp. They wrap the wound, but you've lost too much blood. You die in the jungle, ending your search for Paititi.

THE END

To follow another path, turn to page 11.
To learn more about life in the rain forest, turn to page 101.

Black caimans can grow up to 13 feet long. They don't usually attack humans, but it's not worth the risk.

The next morning, the team continues on in the rain. You huddle miserably in the boats for days. Finally, you land along the riverbank and hike through the jungle. Hour after hour, you hack at vines, scramble over logs, and slap away insects.

• Turn the page.

Eventually, a sheer cliff rises from the jungle. Many carvings cover the base of the rock. You found it!

The team thinks these carved symbols could be a map to Paititi. But no one can decode the ancient writings. You're out of time, supplies, and energy. You have to head back to civilization for now. But you know where to start your search when you come back some day.

THE END

To follow another path, turn to page 11.
To learn more about life in the rain forest, turn to page 101.

It takes the team hours to carry the boats and supplies past the danger. Finally, you reach smoother water and continue the journey. Your guide calmly mentions that this river is home to many piranhas. These water predators have razor-sharp teeth. Red-bellied piranhas are the most dangerous. But piranhas don't usually attack people. Most only eat water animals such as shrimp or other small fish.

You see a huge tree floating in the middle of the river. Before you have time to react, the supply boat crashes into the tree. It spills food and supplies into the dark, muddy water. You only have a few seconds. Do you let the supplies go and save yourself? Or do you try to grab what you can before the current carries it away?

- To let the supplies go, turn to page 30.
- To jump into the water and try to save the supplies, turn to page 32.

Most of your supplies disappear downstream. That night, you make camp. You count the few supplies you have left. Unfortunately, most of the food was lost. The guide makes a surprising suggestion. He wants to fish for piranha!

The guide casts a small net into the water and pulls out several red-bellied piranhas. They flap furiously. You carefully reach out to untangle the net. You get a little too close to one. With a quick move, the fish takes a bite out of your hand. You scream and drop the fish, as the others rush to wrap your wound. It throbs with pain.

By the next morning, your hand is red and swollen. It's infected. You're feverish and dizzy. The guides take you out of the jungle before the infection gets worse. Your search for the Gold City is over.

THE END

To follow another path, turn to page 11.
To learn more about life in the rain forest, turn to page 101.

You jump into the river and grab as many supplies as you can. Somehow, you make it back to the boat. Everyone declares you a hero.

At nightfall, the group makes camp near the riverbank. As you're unloading the boats, you spot some of your supplies floating in the water. You could wade in and get them. But it's dark, and you don't know what's lurking in the water.

- To get the supplies, go to page 33.
- To let them go, turn to page 34.

The water is only about a foot deep here, so you're safe from piranhas. You pile some of the supplies on the ground and reach for more. Suddenly, a jolt throws you off your feet. You've grabbed an electric eel! These long, snake-like animals live in the Amazon Rain Forest.

The shock doesn't kill you, but it packs a powerful punch. You land facedown in the shallow water. You struggle to get your head above the water, but you can't feel your body. The end comes quickly as you drown, your hand still gripping the eel.

THE END

To follow another path, turn to page 11.
To learn more about life in the rain forest, turn to page 101.

It's not worth the risk, so you head back to camp. Two days later, you reach a small fishing village. The team gets needed supplies. Locals tell you about some ruins and artifacts on a mountainside near here. This is the place you were looking for!

Your team soon begins the long climb up the mountain. You find the ruins of a stone pathway, so you follow it. Butterflies dart through the jungle. Monkeys chatter from the trees. That afternoon, the jungle opens up to reveal a maze of vine-covered stone walls. On the walls, you see ancient carvings. Could this be the lost city of Paititi? It's an exciting find, no matter what. The team will stay here as long as they can. You can't wait to uncover more of these hidden ruins in the days to come.

THE END

To follow another path, turn to page 11.
To learn more about life in the rain forest, turn to page 101.

CHAPTER 3

MEDICINE AND ADVENTURE IN THE CONGO

As you step off the small plane, it's hard to believe you're finally in the Congo! This African rain forest covers more than a million square miles. It stretches across six countries. Just think of all the animals you might see—elephants, leopards, and gorillas.

But you're here in search of medicinal plants. There's one special plant you hope to find. It's a type of liana, or climbing vine.

• Turn the page.

Lianas live on rain forest trees. The liana you're looking for could cure a type of cancer. This particular vine is so rare it doesn't even have a name yet. If you could find it, you could save countless lives.

After a two-day trip into the jungle, your team arrives at a small village. You build a base camp. From here, members of your group will fan out into the rain forest to look for plants.

One of the local villagers says he's seen the liana somewhere near the village. He's also seen it near a river about a mile or so through the rain forest.

- To search the nearby jungle, go to page 39.
- To explore the river, turn to page 51.

The world's rain forests could hold more than half of all known species of plants. Several drugs humans use today came from rain forest plants. The drug quinine, for instance, comes from the bark of a rain forest tree. It is used to treat malaria, a deadly disease. But the clearing of the rain forest threatens its precious plants.

You search the thick, green forest carefully. After some time, you hear a crashing noise in the jungle nearby. Something big is out there.

- To see what is making the noise, turn to page 40.
- To quickly move on, turn to page 47.

An animal is pulling down vines and tree branches ahead. It's an elephant. Forest elephants are smaller than other African elephants. Their tusks have a pinkish color to them. This makes these animals targets for poachers. Poachers illegally kill these peaceful creatures for their tusks.

The elephant has a baby at her side. The little forest elephant is pulling a tangle of vines. Watching the playful baby fills you with joy. It makes you even more determined to help save this rain forest.

The baby gets caught in a long vine. It gives out a frustrated squeak. Its mother gently pulls the vine with her trunk. You squint to get a closer look at the vines, and your heart jumps. They may be the vines you're searching for. You need to get a closer look. But you don't want to bother the mother and baby.

• To get closer, go to page 41.
• To leave them alone, turn to page 44.

You take a few steps closer. The mother pauses and looks around, clearly on alert. At first, you're afraid she's spotted you. Then you see movement in the thick jungle between you and the elephant. It's a person you have never seen. He has a large rifle in his hand. It's a poacher here to get the elephant's tusks!

Fortunately, he hasn't seen you. Confronting poachers can be very dangerous. But you can't let him harm the elephants. Maybe you can help the elephants in a different way.

• To stay where you are, turn to page 42.
• To sneak up on the poacher, turn to page 43.

Thinking fast, you get an idea. Elephants are afraid of anything that moves around their feet. This fear is probably where the myth that elephants are afraid of mice comes from. You toss a few small rocks near the elephant's feet. She lets out a bellow and runs straight toward the poacher. The huge animal crashes into him, throwing him several feet into a large tree. The mother and baby escape into the forest.

The poacher lies on the ground, moaning. Villagers and others on your team come running. The local men take the gun and drag the injured poacher to the village to be arrested. You follow them, collecting some of the vines before you go. Even if they aren't what you're looking for, you're happy that you helped the elephant and her baby.

THE END

To follow another path, turn to page 11.
To learn more about life in the rain forest, turn to page 101.

The poacher is too focused on the elephant to hear you. As he raises his gun to shoot, you slam a rock against his head. He crumples to the ground. You don't think he's dead, but he's clearly knocked out. The noise scares the elephant and her baby. They flap their ears and thunder toward you. You have just enough time to jump out of the way, but the poacher doesn't. You run to the village and report that a poacher has been trampled. A group of local men go out to see if he is still alive.

You're glad the elephants are safe, but you feel awful about the poacher. Yes, poaching is a terrible crime, but you didn't want him to be killed. Maybe you could have done something differently? You'll never know.

THE END

To follow another path, turn to page 11.
To learn more about life in the rain forest, turn to page 101.

You venture into the underbrush, scanning the vines and plants. None match the one you're searching for. The jungle opens up onto a beautiful, wide pasture. A network of marshy streams trickles peacefully through green grass. A herd of forest buffalo grazes calmly in the clearing.

You must get a selfie in this perfect African scene. A photo with the buffalo would be great too. Forest buffalo don't look like the America variety, which are actually called bison. African buffalo are smaller, with rust-red coats, and short, curved horns. As you try to figure out the best angle, you notice a movement in the jungle near the edge of the clearing.

- To ignore the movement and get closer to the buffalo, go to page 45.
- To investigate the movement, turn to page 46.

You creep closer and stand under a vine-covered tree, snapping photos as you go. One of the vines drops down behind you, ruining the shot. You reach up to push it away and realize it's not a vine. It's a snake!

You feel its rough, scaly skin as it strikes your hand. Your screams startle the buffalo. They storm into the jungle.

It turns out you've been bitten by a spiny bush viper. That's one of the most venomous snakes in the Congo. It causes internal bleeding. You spend days in agony before you're finally airlifted to a hospital. You can only hope you receive medical care in time to survive.

THE END

To follow another path, turn to page 11.
To learn more about life in the rain forest, turn to page 101.

You inch slowly toward the movement. A creature is sniffing the leaves. It has a narrow head and a long tail. It's covered in hard scales. It digs into a large ant nest with its huge claws. Then it licks up the tiny insects with its long tongue.

You've found a pangolin, or scaly anteater. These creatures are among the most endangered African animals. Poachers trap them for their scales and their meat. When they're afraid, they roll into a ball for protection.

After a few minutes, it wanders into the jungle. As you watch it go, you see the vines you're looking for! You fill your bag with several samples, grateful to the pangolin that attracted you to this spot.

THE END

To follow another path, turn to page 11.
To learn more about life in the rain forest, turn to page 101.

You don't want to know what is making that loud noise. You round a bend in the trail and find a clearing full of gorillas. Two females cradle babies. Several half-grown gorillas tumble and play together. These are eastern lowland gorillas, an endangered gorilla species.

• Turn the page.

You slowly pull out your phone and start taking photos. Then you notice a shadow in the underbrush. The biggest gorilla you've ever seen steps out. The fur on his back is a silvery-grey. A silverback gorilla can be dangerous when it's defending its family. He stands up on two legs and begins to hoot and grunt. Then he rushes straight at you.

- To hold still and stare down the gorilla, go to page 49.
- To crouch and stay still, turn to page 50.

You glare at the gorilla, and he stops. You assume you've shown him who's boss. But then the huge animal lets out an earsplitting roar.

Staring at the gorilla was the wrong thing to do! To him, that was a challenge to fight. You turn and run. The gorilla crashes through the jungle behind you. A powerful blow from behind sends you flying into a tree.

Blinding pain shoots up your leg, and you lose consciousness. When your team finds you later, they can't believe you're alive. Your leg is broken, and you have some deep scrapes.

The team doctor splints your leg. You won't be walking for weeks. All you can do now is stay in camp. Hopefully, someone else will make the discovery you always wanted to make.

THE END

To follow another path, turn to page 11.
To learn more about life in the rain forest, turn to page 101.

You crouch and keep your eyes on the ground. If you make yourself smaller than the gorilla, he will see that you are no threat.

The huge silverback stops, puzzled. He is more than twice your size. He could smash your skull with one punch. You hold your breath. He reaches out and gently touches your head.

One by one, the other gorillas come to you. One of the babies takes your hand. For several minutes, the gorilla family greets you. Then they turn and walk into the jungle.

You sit in the clearing for a long time, stunned at this incredible encounter. It's an experience you'll never forget.

THE END

To follow another path, turn to page 11.
To learn more about life in the rain forest, turn to page 101.

It's a hot, steamy morning as you and Andre, one of your teammates, set out for the river. This area of the Congo is known as the Congo River Basin. It stretches for 1.3 million square miles in Africa. This land is a huge network of rivers, streams, swamps, forests, and grasslands.

The Congo River Basin has more than 10,000 species of plants. Almost one-third of them can't be found anywhere else on Earth. You're hoping one of them is the liana you're looking for.

Andre is on the lookout for any signs of predators. The local villagers have warned you of a dangerous leopard in the area. They haven't seen it in a while. Andre hopes it's gone farther into the jungle.

• Turn the page.

You reach the small river and carefully look around. A flock of gray parrots chatter and flit among the trees. A particularly loud one sits on a thick vine. Looking closer, you think it might be the vine you're searching for.

Andre calls to you from the riverbank. He's found a set of tracks in the mud. They look like they could be from a leopard. Andre isn't sure how old the tracks are. He thinks you should follow them. He wants to make sure the animal has left for good and that you're safe.

- To look at the vines in the tree, turn to page 54.
- To follow the tracks, turn to page 62.

You haven't climbed a tree in a while, but you manage to get up to the vines. After cutting a few samples, you pause to look around. It's beautiful up here. The sunlight filters through the thick forest canopy. The air is filled with the sounds of birds and buzzing insects. The world feels alive, and you love it.

A nearby tree is heavy with mafambu, a forest fruit about the size of an orange. As you reach for one, you see a bonobo in the tree. Bonobos are a smaller species of chimpanzee. This one is eating a mafambu.

You hold your breath as she gazes at you calmly. Then she reaches out and hands you a piece of fruit. You take it, trying not to smile. Showing your teeth is a sign of anger to bonobos. Then she slowly climbs along the branch and disappears into the canopy. You watch her go, moved by this unexpected encounter.

As you carefully climb back down, you don't notice another bonobo on the ground. As your feet touch the earth, the bonobo gives a loud screech and hits you. You should have known to look out for them. Like most apes, bonobos live in groups.

- To remain still, turn to page 56.
- To run away, turn to page 58.

Standing still was a mistake. The animal jumps onto your shoulders. He grabs your arms and bites you around the face and neck. You scream in pain, and the bonobo runs off.

Andre rushes to your side and helps you back to camp. The villagers tell you you're not the first person attacked by them. The local bonobo group is very aggressive.

The team doctor stitches the wounds, but one bite is especially bad. You must have surgery immediately. Sadly, you leave, hoping to come back one day.

THE END

To follow another path, turn to page 11.
To learn more about life in the rain forest, turn to page 101.

You don't wait to see what this large, aggressive male bonobo is going to do. You back away quickly, then run. The animal is right behind you all the way to the river. You jump into the water, knowing bonobos don't like to swim. The male stops at the bank, jumping and drumming the ground with his fists. The churning water swiftly carries you downstream.

Something bumps your leg, and you think it's a log. Then an enormous hippo rises out of the muddy water. You could try to swim around the hippo and escape back to the riverbank. Or you could let the current carry you away.

- To swim to shore, go to page 59.
- To let the current carry you downstream, turn to page 61.

You frantically swim toward the shore. The hippo is right behind you as you stumble out of the water and scramble up the steep, muddy bank. Something sharp stabs your leg, and you wince. You're not sure what it was, but you don't let it slow you down. The mud slips and slides under your feet. You feel as though you'll never get to the top of the riverbank.

When you finally do, a loud rumble explodes behind you. You look back. A large section of the dirt, mud, and underbrush has broken away and fallen into the river below.

It looks like the hippo had the same problems that you did. It must have lost its balance on the slippery bank and fallen back into the water. You hope it's okay, but you're relieved that you seem to be out of harm's way, at least for now.

• Turn the page.

You do your best to stumble back to camp, while blood streams from the gash in your leg. When you finally get there, you're barely alive. You managed to survive your animal encounters, but your scientific adventure in the Congo is over.

THE END

To follow another path, turn to page 11.
To learn more about life in the rain forest, turn to page 101.

The hippo lunges as you frantically swim, letting the current push you. Male hippos can weigh more than two tons, but they're fast in the water. Then you feel a pressure around your legs. *They're in the hippo's mouth!* It's your last thought as the hippo pulls you under the dark, muddy water.

THE END

To follow another path, turn to page 11.
To learn more about life in the rain forest, turn to page 101.

It's rare to see a leopard in the Congo Rain Forest. These big cats spend most of their time in trees. They come out at night to hunt.

Eventually, the tracks disappear. Andre thinks the leopard has left the area. You're relieved that it's gone. You feel safe enough to separate and collect plant samples.

But as it turns out, Andre was wrong. He calls out and motions toward a clump of underbrush. Two tiny leopard cubs are sleeping beneath it. Fear lurches in your stomach. Female leopards hide their cubs when they go hunting. The mother is surely close by. You need to get out of here. Andre knows it isn't safe to be here, either. But he's excited to see that the leopard population is growing. That's good news for the rain forest. He wants to take a couple of quick photos as proof before you leave.

• To leave quickly, go to page 63.
• To stay with Andre, turn to page 64.

This is a bad idea, but Andre won't listen to you. You get some distance between you and the cubs, hoping Andre comes soon. After several minutes, a scream rips through the forest. You race back to see Andre on the ground and a large, snarling leopard on top of him. You grab a thick branch and swing it at the animal. It jumps away and pauses, hissing and growling. It's the chance you need to grab Andre's legs and drag him away. You expect an attack from the leopard any second, but she watches until you're gone.

Andre is alive. But he's bleeding from several deep scratches and a bite on his arm. The next day, the injuries become swollen and infected. He has to be airlifted to the nearest hospital. You're thankful he wasn't killed but sorry he'll miss the rest of the expedition.

THE END

To follow another path, turn to page 11.
To learn more about life in the rain forest, turn to page 101.

Andre snaps a few pictures while your eyes dart back and forth, looking for the mama leopard. Finally, he's done. You both turn and are shocked to see a large female leopard standing about 20 feet away.

Your first instinct is to run, but that's not smart. Leopards are great runners. She would catch you in an instant. Instead, you want to look large and intimidating, so she'll leave you alone. Together, you start yelling and waving your hands in the air, all the time walking backward. It works! She watches as you stumble through the underbrush. When you're out of her sight, you both turn and run.

After a time, you stop to catch your breath. You're lucky that the leopard didn't follow. Neither of you feels safe in the jungle now, so you return to camp. The others can't believe you encountered a leopard and lived. You can't either.

THE END

To follow another path, turn to page 11.
To learn more about life in the rain forest, turn to page 101.

CHAPTER 4

PROTECTING ENDANGERED RAIN FOREST ANIMALS

When you were small, you saw a documentary on the rain forests of the Indonesian island of Sumatra. The green forests and mysterious animals captured your imagination. Now you're traveling to Sumatra as part of a scientific expedition. The team's job is to locate a serow, a rare and endangered animal.

• Turn the page.

Once, the Sumatran Rain Forest covered
most of the island. Over the last 20 years, more
than 29.7 million acres have been destroyed.
Today, only a few patchy areas survive. Most of
the remaining rain forests are national parks.
But even those are being illegally cut down.
Some scientists think that all the Sumatran
Rain Forest will be gone in just a few years.

The Sumatran Rain Forest is the only place in the world where elephants, orangutans, tigers, and rhinos all live together. Habitat loss isn't the only danger to these animals. The rain forests that are left are surrounded by farms and towns. The animals can't travel to other rain forest areas to find mates.

The situation in Sumatra makes you want to save the rain forests and the animals. The serow is one of them. No one knows much about this goat-like animal. But you think the serow might be an important part of the diets of larger predators like tigers. By studying prey animals, you will find out how the rain forest ecosystem works. You might even be lucky enough to encounter other endangered animals while you're here too.

• Turn the page.

You arrive and check into the hotel. Tomorrow, the team will split up. One group will head to Kerinci Seblat National Park to set up camera traps. Hopefully, these cameras will capture photos of a serow. The other team will leave for Gunung Leuser National Park. The rangers have reported sightings of serows in the mountainous areas of the park. This team's mission is to find and observe serows in their rain forest habitat.

• To join the team setting up camera traps, go to page 71.
• To head to the mountains, turn to page 86.

The research station will be home for the next few weeks. You want to set up dozens of camera traps in different sections of the park. These small cameras take photos of any animal that passes by. The photos and video they capture will give scientists information about the rain forest animals.

The next day, you head into the jungle. After some hiking, you find a narrow path through the underbrush. It's the perfect place for a camera trap. You attach it to a tree with a strap. As you tighten the strap, you sense something watching you.

The hairs on your neck prickle with fear. Slowly, you turn around. A Sumatran tiger is staring at you from the underbrush.

• Turn the page.

These tigers, with their thick black stripes, are the smallest tiger species in the world. But that doesn't mean they're small. They can grow to more than 250 pounds and be as long as 8 feet. They also have webbed toes, which make them great swimmers. Only 400 to 600 Sumatran tigers remain in the wild, and they all live here.

The tiger stares at you, and you don't move. There have been several reports of tiger attacks in the area. After a few moments, the tiger disappears into the jungle. You notice what looks like blood on its beautiful fur. An injured animal can be very dangerous. But the tiger might be injured and need help. You could follow the tiger to see if you could help it in some way.

• To continue your work, turn to page 74.
• To follow the tiger, turn to page 80.

It's very rare to see a Sumatran tiger, especially so close. They're solitary, shy animals that usually sleep during the day.

You notice several tiger tracks on the path. A nearby tree has scratch marks on the trunk. These are clues that the tiger comes here often.

To your relief you don't see any blood on the ground. Maybe it was mud on its fur. You're hopeful that the camera will take photos of the beautiful, rare animal. The photos could show if the tiger is injured or not.

Once you've calmed down, you continue on through the jungle. You don't see any more signs of the tiger. You begin to relax.

You're on the lookout for creeks, streams, and animal paths. These are good spots for a camera because animals visit them often. As you set another camera trap, you hear a rustling in the underbrush nearby.

• To check out the rustling, turn to page 76.
• To ignore it, turn to page 77.

You pull back the underbrush. You're shocked to see a sun bear. With their thick, black fur, sun bears are the world's smallest bear. Their huge claws help them climb rain forest trees. They also have the longest tongues of any bear species. They stick them into insect nests for tasty treats.

One of the bear's paws is caught in a trap. Many local farmers think sun bears are pests. They kill the bears to protect crops. You take a knife from your backpack and cut the trap away from the bear's paw. The animal stands up and slowly climbs a nearby tree.

You put the trap in your pack. You'll need it as proof when you report this illegal trapping to the park authorities. It's a relief that the bear is okay, and you're glad you could help it.

THE END

To follow another path, turn to page 11.
To learn more about life in the rain forest, turn to page 101.

You don't want to disturb whatever animal is in the underbrush, so you continue on. The rain forest is especially beautiful today. The jungle hums with birdcalls and buzzing insects. Above, branches sway as squirrels jump from tree to tree. You spot a huge lizard called a water monitor. It is sunning itself on a log near a stream.

After setting up another camera trap, you move on to a promising site near a creek. Up ahead, a dark shadow moves through the underbrush. It might be a serow! You could be one of the few scientists to observe a serow in the wild. But if you get too close it could run away for good.

• To get closer, turn to page 78.
• To leave the animal alone, turn to page 79.

You carefully creep closer, your phone ready to take as many photos as you can. Then the animal's head appears out of the underbrush. It's not a serow after all. It's a Malayan tapir. These anteater-like animals have black fur on their front and back, with a stripe of white fur in the middle. This one looks to be more than 500 pounds!

For a moment, you and the startled tapir stand face-to-face. Suddenly, the frightened animal crashes forward and knocks you to the ground. Then it disappears into the rain forest.

You sit up, gasping. The animal knocked the wind out of you. You're relieved that you're not hurt. But you're ashamed that you disturbed this rain forest animal.

THE END

To follow another path, turn to page 11.
To learn more about life in the rain forest, turn to page 101.

You don't want to risk scaring the animal away, so you leave as quietly as you can. A week later, you make your way back through the rain forest. You check every trap and download the images and video from each camera.

That night, the team reviews the footage. Some of the cameras recorded tigers and tapirs, and one even caught a photo of an elephant. The best video shows a pair of serows walking up to one of the camera traps!

You're thrilled! It's the first proof of serows in this part of the rain forest. Maybe you'll be lucky enough to see one in the wild before this research trip is over.

THE END

To follow another path, turn to page 11.
To learn more about life in the rain forest, turn to page 101.

You head in the same direction as the tiger. Carefully, you scan the jungle floor. No signs of blood. You begin to calm down. Then you hear the sound of water. The path ends at a large pool. A beautiful waterfall cascades down a tall cliff. A group of Sumatran elephants are peacefully gathered in the pool. You watch the elephants as they drink and bathe, throwing water onto their backs with their strong trunks.

These endangered elephants are very important to the rain forest ecosystem. They eat many kinds of plants. The seeds from the plants end up in the elephant's dung. They spread their dung throughout the jungle. This allows the jungle to grow and thrive. Sadly, there are fewer than 3,000 elephants left. The biggest threat they face is habitat loss.

Suddenly, you hear a low rumble. It is a warning sound from the leader. The elephants rush out of the pool. You must have frightened them. You're disappointed that you disturbed the elephants. Then you remember the tiger. Fear turns in your stomach. But there isn't any sign of the tiger here. You can stay and set up a camera at the pool. Or you can leave with the elephants.

• To stay at the pool, turn to page 82.
• To follow the elephant herd, turn to page 83.

You see a good place to set the camera. As you work, you relax. The cool mist of the waterfall hits your face. Birds chirp and sing in the trees. Spots of sunlight glisten on a huge fallen log nearby. When you are finished, you sit down on the log. You pull a canteen from your pack and take a long drink. It's time to get back to camp.

You stand up and turn. A blur of gold and black fur leaps toward you. You fall into the pool, gasping. The huge tiger lands on top of you, and you quickly drown. The team doesn't know what happened to you. They can't find your body. Then they think to check the camera trap. The video on the camera shows exactly how you died in the rain forest.

THE END

To follow another path, turn to page 11.
To learn more about life in the rain forest, turn to page 101.

You manage to follow the elephants for a time. Then the jungle begins to thin. You see farm fields through the trees. You start to panic. As the Sumatran rain forest is destroyed, the elephants look for food on the farms. Farmers don't want elephants to eat their crops. Many of them put out poison.

• Turn the page.

Maybe you can keep the herd from getting near the farms. Thinking quickly, you jump out and wave your arms. You want to scare the elephants away from the fields. With a bellow, the lead elephant turns and thunders back into the jungle. The rest of the herd follows her. It worked!

Then a gunshot echoes through the forest. You feel a searing pain in your side. Soon, you're surrounded by a group of people who shout "pemburu gelap!" That means poacher in Indonesian. They think you're a poacher trying to illegally harm the elephants. You try to explain, but it's too late.

THE END

To follow another path, turn to page 11.
To learn more about life in the rain forest, turn to page 101.

The biggest remaining patch of Sumatran Rain Forest includes Gunung Leuser National Park. It stretches for about 2 million acres in the northern area of Indonesia. You know that serows live there. Camera traps have taken pictures of them on the mountain. Your job now is to find a live serow in the wild. You are also here to study the plants and animals in the serow's habitat.

Hiking through the jungle, you scan the ground for serow dung. Every animal's dung looks different. Serows mark their territory with small dung piles. As you trek deeper into the jungle, you spot one! But the dung is old and dry. This means the serow hasn't been in this area for a while.

Then you see a pile of dung that makes your heart stop. It's Sumatran rhinoceros dung, and it's fresh.

Sumatran rhinos are some of the most critically endangered animals in the world. There are fewer than 80 of them left in the wild, and they all live in the Sumatran Rain Forest.

• To follow the rhino dung, turn to page 88.
• To look for more serow dung, turn to page 94.

Sumatran rhinoceroses used to live throughout Indonesia. Now the island of Sumatra is one of the only places they live. The rhinos are separated into small groups. Each group lives in a different national park. This makes it almost impossible for them to find mates. Sadly, poachers still hunt these rhinos too.

A noise in the jungle makes you stop. Sumatran rhinos are huge animals. They can be dangerous when frightened. They are the smallest rhino species, but they can grow up to 2,000 pounds. They are also covered in fuzzy hair. No other rhinos have that much hair. The hair gets filled with mud. This mud helps the rhino's skin stay cool. It also keeps insects away.

You hear voices. Four people are moving in the brush ahead. Quickly, you duck, hoping they didn't see you. If they're poachers, you could be in as much danger as the rhino. Poaching is illegal, and they don't want to get caught.

• To follow the group, turn to page 90.
• To slip away, turn to page 93.

You follow the poachers. You don't notice that one has stepped out of the group. He creeps up behind you. He shouts and points a gun. Heart pounding, you raise your hands as the other three men surround you.

When you explain who you are, they lower their weapons. To your surprise they're not poachers. This group is a Rhino Protection Unit. Rhino Protection Units were created to protect the few wild Sumatran rhinos. Each four-person unit patrols the rain forest. They search for rhinos and arrest poachers.

You tell them about the rhino dung. They get very excited. They tell you that they've spotted serow dung not far from here. They invite you to come with them on their rhino search.

• To go with the Rhino Protection Unit, go to page 91.
• To follow the serow, turn to page 92.

You like the idea of being protected in the jungle, so you go with the rangers. One of them suddenly stops. He motions you forward. Slowly, you step through the thick underbrush. You're holding your breath with excitement. You peer through the trees. A large rhino is standing in a shallow creek. She is calmly pulling leaves from a tree. Your eyes blur with tears of joy to see this rare and amazing animal. You all stand in silent awe as the rhino finishes her meal. Slowly, she ambles into the jungle.

You had set out in search of serow, but you've experienced something almost as rare. You are now one of the few humans who has ever seen a Sumatran rhino in the wild. It is an encounter you will remember for the rest of your life.

THE END

To follow another path, turn to page 11.
To learn more about life in the rain forest, turn to page 101.

It is tempting to have the protection of the rangers. But you need to stay focused. You find the serow dung exactly where the rangers said it would be. You follow the dung piles. You write down the location of each one. You chuckle at the idea that animal poop could be so exciting.

Finally, the jungle opens into a wide mountain clearing. Far above, a movement catches your eye. There, scrambling over some rocks, is a herd of serows! You note where you are and how many animals you see. Of course, you take some photos too.

The herd grazes for a few minutes then moves away. Once they're gone, you almost can't believe you saw them. You can't wait to return tomorrow and begin your study of these rain forest animals.

THE END

To follow another path, turn to page 11.
To learn more about life in the rain forest, turn to page 101.

You hike back to the research station as quickly as you can. Then you radio into the park ranger station. You have to report these poachers!

To your shock, the park ranger laughs. She explains that the people you saw were Rhino Protection Unit rangers. Rhino Protection Units travel through the rain forest, searching for rhinos, destroying traps, and arresting poachers. Since the Rhino Protection Units were created over 20 years ago, there have only been five rhino poachings.

You feel better after speaking to the park ranger. Tomorrow, when you return to the rain forest, you won't make the same mistake.

THE END

To follow another path, turn to page 11.
To learn more about life in the rain forest, turn to page 101.

You didn't come here to look for Sumatran rhinos, so you continue on. You walk the area, but all you find is more dry serow dung. Even though you're disappointed, it's encouraging to know the animals have been in the area.

Suddenly, a buzzing sound draws your attention. A swarm of flies and insects seem to be covering something. Excitedly, you rush over and take a look, hoping it's fresh serow dung. But it's only a pile of sticky, half-eaten figs.

You look up and see a large orangutan sitting in the crook of the tree. A tiny baby orangutan clings to her back. They both gaze at you as the mother nibbles a piece of fruit.

• To stay and watch the orangutans, go to page 95.
• To leave the animals alone, turn to page 96.

Orangutans live throughout the Sumatran rain forest. Their name means "person of the forest." They have deep red fur. They also have very long arms and legs, which let them climb expertly through the trees. These animals rarely come this close to the forest floor. The beautiful female moves across a large branch toward you. She reaches out and touches your cheek. Slowly, you stroke her rough, red fur.

After a moment, she turns and climbs upward. They disappear into the lush, green rain forest canopy. You watch them go, overwhelmed by this encounter. You're still looking for scrow, but your encounter with your ape friend might be what you remember most from this trip.

THE END

To follow another path, turn to page 11.
To learn more about life in the rain forest, turn to page 101.

You're surprised to see an orangutan so close to the rain forest floor. They like to stay high in the rain forest canopy. She calmly pulls a fig from a nearby branch. Then you understand why they are here. This tree is loaded with ripe fruit. Orangutans eat hundreds of different jungle fruits. They spread the seeds of these plants in their dung. This allows healthy plants to grow everywhere.

You take several photos and make careful notes about your location. Then you continue your search.

The path continues upward. You climb higher into the mountains. Finally, you spot a pile of fresh serow dung. You're getting closer!

There's also fresh tracks near the dung. The tracks were made by a large cat. It's going to be dark soon. You really want to find the serow. But you don't want to be in the jungle at night.

• To continue up the path, turn to page 98.
• To head back to the research station, turn to page 99.

You can't turn back when you're this close! It's almost dark when you see a shocking sight. A dead, half-eaten serow lies in the underbrush near the path. You get closer and see it's a fresh kill. Whatever got this serow is probably still nearby.

Suddenly, a heavy weight hits your back. You shake it off, screaming. You whirl around and see a Sumatran tiger crouching near the dead serow. Before you can move, the tiger leaps, and this time its fangs sink into your neck. You don't blame the tiger for protecting its prey. You should have gone back to camp when you had the chance.

THE END

To follow another path, turn to page 11.
To learn more about life in the rain forest, turn to page 101.

You take note of your location and plan to come back. Better safe than sorry. As the sun begins to set, you reach a deep creek. As you try to figure out how to cross it, a movement near the water catches your eye. You stand still, barely breathing. A dark goat-like head pops out of the underbrush. Another one joins it. Serows! You do your best not to move as the two serows bend down and drink. Then they quickly disappear into the underbrush. You can't believe it!

You make it back and excitedly tell the others what you saw. They're as thrilled as you are. You can't wait to return to the creek. With any luck, you'll see these rare animals again.

THE END

To follow another path, turn to page 11.
To learn more about life in the rain forest, turn to page 101.

CHAPTER 5

PROTECTING RAIN FORESTS

The tropical rain forest is one of the most important ecosystems in the world. Rain forests grow on every continent except Antarctica. An ecosystem must have three things to be a true rain forest. It must have very tall, strong trees. It has to get a lot of rain. And it must be in a place with high temperatures. These conditions are perfect around the equator, so most of the world's rain forests are found there.

Stories of deadly rain forest animals grip our imagination. Most of these ideas come from books, movies, and other media. The reality is much more complicated. It's true that rain forests can be dangerous places. An unexpected encounter with a rain forest animal could be deadly.

Until recently, most rain forest encounters between humans and animals were rare. But as humans have destroyed the rain forests, things have changed. Roads now cut through areas that were once impassible. Villages and farms sit in places once covered by jungle. The animals that used to live in these areas now must share their homes with humans. This doesn't always go well.

Near Sumatra's national parks, tiger attacks have become a problem for farmers. Tigers attack and kill livestock, such as cows, for food. The farmers kill the tigers to protect their farms.

In Africa, villages around Lake Olbolosat in Kenya are threatened by hippos in the nearby lake. The local government dug a trench between the lake and the villages to keep the hippos away.

Most rain forest animals are not a threat to humans. In fact, encountering a wild animal in its habitat can be an awe-inspiring experience. Follow a few basic rules during an animal encounter to keep both you and the animal safe.

Most importantly, respect the animal's space. Stay a good distance away from an animal to make sure it doesn't feel trapped. Don't ever try to touch or pet a wild animal, and don't follow or chase it if it starts to leave. Adult animals are especially protective of their young, so if you see a baby, stay away. Never feed a wild animal. By following these rules, most people who interact with these animals can have a safe and thrilling once-in-a-lifetime encounter.

John J. King II

In 2011, John J. King II, an American tourist, had an unexpected encounter during his visit to a safari camp in the African rain forests of Uganda. An entire family of gorillas, including an enormous male silverback, gathered around King. King crouched with his camera. The silverback sat behind him as the curious babies climbed on his head, touching and sniffing him. After a few minutes, the family wandered back into the jungle. The video of King's once-in-a-lifetime encounter went viral.

Kristen Yaldor

In 2018, American Kristen Yaldor was kayaking in Zimbabwe, Africa. A hippo upended her kayak, throwing her into the water. As she swam to escape, the hippo attacked. Yaldor suffered several injuries but survived.

South Sumatra Attacks

In 2019, two tiger attacks shook South Sumatra. During the first attack, a group of tourists were camping on a tea plantation. The tiger attacked the group. One tourist was badly injured but survived. The next day, a Sumatran coffee farmer was in his fields, cutting a tree. Without warning, a Sumatran tiger appeared and attacked. The farmer fought with the tiger, but he was killed. The tiger escaped back into the jungle and was never caught.

This book placed you in wildlife encounters in the rain forest. Think about these other situations.

You live in a village deep in the rain forest. Your people get food, water, and medicine from the rain forest. But there are few jobs in your village. One day, a man arrives. His company wants to build a farm nearby. The villagers could get jobs cutting down trees. When the trees are gone, they can work on the farm. Some villagers are excited about the jobs. Others don't want the rain forests cut down. Which side are you on?

You work in a world-class zoo breeding endangered animals. You hope to free them back into the wild. But many captive-bred animals don't know how to survive in the wild. Is it right to save these animals if they have to live in cages?

You have been offered a job as a tour guide in a rain forest park. You're excited because this park practices ecotourism. Ecotourism wants visitors to be respectful of animals and people in ecosystems like rain forests. Your job will be to take tourists into the rain forest to see the animals that live there. The company promises that the tourists will see animals like gorillas, tigers, and jaguars. This means you will have to drive cars into fragile areas of the rain forest. The cars could scare the animals and damage their habitat. But the money from the tourists will be used to protect the park and its wildlife. Do you think it is worth the risk to the animals?

GLOSSARY

continent (KAHN-tuh-nuhnt)—one of Earth's seven large land masses

ecosystem (EE-koh-sis-tuhm)—a group of animals and plants that work together with their surroundings

ecotourism (ek-oh-TOOR-iz-uhm)—visiting a place that has unspoiled natural resources, while being careful to have minimal impact on the environment

endangered (in-DAYN-juhrd)—at risk of dying out

habitat (HAB-uh-tat)—the natural place and conditions in which a plant or animal lives

liana (lee-AH-nuh)—a woody vine found in tropical rain forests

paralysis (puh-RAL-uh-sis)—the loss of movement

poacher (POHCH-ur)—a person who hunts or fishes illegally

predator (PRED-uh-tur)—an animal that hunts other animals for food

prey (PRAY)—an animal hunted by other animals as food

species (SPEE-sheez)—a group of animals that are biologically similar

underbrush (UHN-der-brush)—shrubs and small trees forming the undergrowth in a forest

venomous (VEN-uh-muhs)—able to produce a poison called venom

BIBLIOGRAPHY

Live Science
livescience.com/congo-river.html

National Geographic
nationalgeographic.org/encyclopedia/rain-forest/

UNESCO
whc.unesco.org/en/list/1167/

World Wildlife Fund
worldwildlife.org

READ MORE

Kenney, Karen Latchana. *Rain Forests.* Hopkins, MN: Bellwether Media, 2021.

Munro, Roxie. *Anteaters, Bats & Boas: The Amazon Rainforest from the Forest Floor to the Treetops.* New York: Holiday House, 2021.

Wilsher, Jane. *Jungle Animals: A Spotter's Guide.* New York: Simon & Schuster, 2021.

Woolf, Alex. *All the Way Down: Amazon Rainforest.* London: Book House, 2021.

INTERNET SITES

National Geographic Kids: Rainforest Habitat
kids.nationalgeographic.com/nature/habitats/article/rain-forest

WorldAtlas
worldatlas.com

World Wildlife Fund
worldwildlife.org

Allison Lassieur is an award-winning author of more than 150 history and nonfiction books about everything from Ancient Rome to the International Space Station. Her books have received several Kirkus starred reviews and Booklist recommendations, and her historical novel *Journey to a Promised Land* was awarded the 2020 Kansas Library Association Notable Book Award and Library of Congress Great Reads Book selection. Allison lives in upstate New York with her husband, daughter, a scruffy, lovable mutt named Jingle Jack, and more books than she can count.